Table Of Contents

Introduction

Artificial intelligence is enchanting field. It brings out a lot of interest in people. There are a lot of blind beliefs surrounding AI. Some pessimistic people feel that artificial intelligence will replace humans, create job loss, and rule over humans. Other optimistic people believe that it's the path to some of the best new opportunities. We just have begun our journey of exploring AI and what it can achieve. We now have the ability to find patterns that only a few decades ago would have been impossible to see. You can also see how AI technologies are becoming more like us. . This book is for managers, entrepreneurs, students, or business professionals who want to better understand how AI technologies might impact their field. You'll see conceptually how each AI approach works for a particular challenge. That way, you can think about the best approach for your new product, project, or even as a starting point for your career.

What is AI?

It is the science and engineering of making intelligent machines. IT is not like the natural intelligence displayed by humans and animals, which involves consciousness and emotionality. It is related to the similar task of using computers to understand human intelligence.

What AI can do?

In less than a decade AI can recognize objects in images, translate languages, speak, navigate maps, predict crop yields, use visual data analysis to clarify disease diagnoses, verify user identity, prepare documents, make lending decisions in financial management translating languages, and transcribing speech. They can outplay humans at complicated strategy games, create photorealistic images, and suggest useful replies to your emails.

What AI cannot do?

Artificial intelligence is not smart enough for cause and effect. We humans also have trouble with it.AI can only do what it is repeatedly taught. They can be trained to identify a Cat but if a Dog is to be included it has to be trained all over again. A self-driving car gets flummoxed by a scenario that a human driver could handle easily.AI cannot tackle situations for which it is not trained for. This problem is called "catastrophic forgetting." Tasks where human creativity is involved AI underperforms, like composing a good song, saying no to children as it is designed to complete preprogramed tasks rather than to think like Humans.

Can AI reach human-level intelligence?

Many people think that human-level intelligence can be achieved by writing large numbers of programs, which can replicate human behaviour and simultaneously new hardware to complement the programs need to be developed .However, most AI researchers believe that new fundamental ideas are required, and therefore it cannot be predicted when human-level intelligence will be achieved.

Common Terminologies Used in AI

Algorithm:
A set of rules that a machine can follow to learn how to do a task.

Backward Chaining:
A Method where the model starts with the desired output and works to find data that might support it.

Big Data:
Datasets that are too large or complex to be used by traditional data processing applications.

Bounding Box:
Commonly used in image or video tagging, this is an imaginary box drawn on an image. The contents of the box are labeled to help a model recognize it as a distinct type of object.

Cognitive Computing:
This is effectively another way to say artificial intelligence. It's used by marketing teams at some companies to avoid the science fiction aura that sometimes surrounds AI.

Data Mining:
The process of analyzing datasets in order to discover new patterns that might improve the model.

Deep Learning:
A function of artificial intelligence that imitates the human brain by learning from the way data is structured, rather than from an algorithm that's programmed to do one specific thing.

Hyper parameter:
Occasionally used interchangeably with parameter, although the terms have some subtle differences. Hyper parameters are values that affect the way your model learns. They are usually set manually outside the model.

Neural Network:

Also called a neural net, this is a computer system designed to function like the human brain. Although researchers are still working on creating a machine model of the human brain, existing neural networks can perform many tasks involving speech, vision and board game strategy.

Natural Language Generation (NLG):

This refers to the process by which a machine turns structured data into text or speech that humans can understand. Essentially, NLG is concerned with what a machine writes or says itself as the end part of the communication process.

Over Fitting:

An important AI term, overfitting is a symptom of machine learning training in which an algorithm is only able to work on or identify specific examples present in the training data. A working model should be able to use the general trends behind the data to work on new examples.

Predictive Analytics:
By combining data mining and machine learning, this type of analytics is built to forecast what will happen within a given timeframe based on historical data and trends.

Supervised Learning:
This is a type of machine learning where structured datasets, with inputs and labels, are used to train and develop an algorithm.

Test Data:
The unlabeled data used to check that a machine learning model is able to perform its assigned task.

Raining Data:
This refers to all the data used during the process of training a machine learning algorithm, as well as the specific dataset used for training rather than testing.

Natural Language Processing (NLP):
The umbrella term for any machine's ability to perform conversational tasks, such as recognizing what is said to it, understanding the intended meaning and responding intelligibly.

Natural Language Understanding (NLU):
As a subset of NLP, this deals with helping machines to recognize the intended meaning of language, taking into account its subtle nuances and any grammatical errors.

Parameter:
A variable inside the model that helps it to make predictions. Their value can be estimated using data and they are usually not set by the person running the model.

Pattern Recognition:
The distinction between this and machine learning is often blurry, but this field is basically concerned with finding trends and patterns in data.

Reinforcement Learning:

This is a method of teaching AI which sets a goal that doesn't have specific metrics, encouraging the model to test different scenarios rather than find a single answer. Based on human feedback, the model can then manipulate the next scenario to get better results

Semantic Annotation:

Tagging different search queries or products with the goal of improving the relevance of a search engine.

Semantic Analysis:

The process of identifying and categorizing opinions in a piece of text, often with the goal of determining the writer's attitude towards something.

Turing Test:

Named after Alan Turing, this tests a machine's ability to pass for a human, particularly in the fields of language and behavior. After being graded by a human, the machine passes if its output is indistinguishable from that of human participants in the test.

Unsupervised Learning:
This is a form of training where the algorithm is asked to make inferences from datasets that don't contain labels. These inferences are what help it to learn.

Validation Data:
 Structured like training data with an input and labels, this data is used to test a recently trained model against new data and to analyze performance, with a particular focus on checking for overfitting.

Variance:
The amount that the intended function of a machine learning model changes while it's being trained. Despite being flexible, models with high variance are prone to overfitting and low predictive accuracy, since they are reliant on their training data.

How to identify A problem in Your Organization

In any organization what are the activities that can be taken over by AI. They can be identified as follows

Process Automation:
Automation of digital and Physical tasks. Identify repetitive tasks that human's do that can be automated. Example Updating customer files with address changes or service additions Reconciliation of data in billing systems to charge or give discounts to customers reading legal and contractual documents to extract provisions using natural language processing.

Cognitive Insight In Sales:
Detect patterns in vast volumes of data and interpret their meaning.
Example:
- Automate personalized targeting of digital ads

- Predict what a particular customer is likely to buy.

Cognitive Engagement:
Automated response to Queries.
Example:
- Use of Chat BOLTS.
- Internal sites for answering employee questions on topics including IT, employee benefits, and HR policy.

9 Steps to Adopting Artificial Intelligence in Your Business

 After identifying the Activities how to go about building the AI for it.

Get Familiar with AI
 Get to know what Hardware software and Human Resources will be required to develop AI

Identify the Problems You Want AI to Solve
See the repetitive tasks in your organization that can be done by AI.

Prioritize Tasks
Identify what can be achieved in short term and long term. See the financial gains in doing so. Example use of BOLTS.

Identify Gap in Capability

What you need to acquire and any processes that need to be internally evolved before you get going. Depending on the business, there may be existing projects or teams that can help do this organically for certain business units.

Bring in Experts and Setup a Pilot Project

Identify the areas where tasks can be outsourced to experts. Develop a test model of your problem that needs to be solved.

Data Integration Normalize the Data

It means identify the data that is useful for the particular problem Start with small dataset Start small and see the results and develop on it.

Data Storage

AI requires lot of Data to learn. As you migrate from pilot to actual your data will grow. So plan for the growth in storage.

AI in Daily Tasks

Educate employees how AI will help them to do their tasks more efficiently and will not be a threat to their employment.

Build With Balance

When designing solutions one must factor in limitations of Hardware, Network. So that optimal solution can be designed. With large amounts of data moving we also need to consider Data security as a part of the solution.

5 important steps to build an AI Project

Data Collection
It is the Procedure of collecting, measuring and analyzing accurate insights for research using standard validated techniques.
Data Collection can be done in 2 ways:
Primary Data: It is raw data that is fresh and is collected for the first time.
Secondary Data: It is previously collected and Tested Data.

Method of Collection:
- Published literature sources
- Surveys (email and mail)
- Interviews (telephone, face-to-face or focus group)
- Observations
- Documents and records
- Experiments

Data Normalization

 Normalization makes sure that all of your data looks and reads the same way across all records.

Methods of Data normalization

<u>Decimal Scaling</u>

It normalizes by moving the decimal point of values of the data. To normalize the data by this technique, we divide each value of the data by the maximum absolute value of data

<u>Min Max Normalization</u>

Min-max normalization is one of the most common ways to normalize data. For every feature, the minimum value of that feature gets transformed into a 0, the maximum value gets transformed into a 1, and every other value gets transformed into a decimal between 0 and 1.

For example, if the minimum value of a feature was 30, and the maximum value was 50, then 40 would be transformed to about 0.5 since it is halfway between 30 and 50. The formula is as follows:

Value-min/max-min

Downside of this Method is that it does not handle outlines very well.

Z-score Normalization

The z-score enables a data administrator to compare two different scores that are from different normal distributions of the data

The formula used for Z-score normalization is below:

Value- μ/σ

Here, μ is the mean value of the feature and σ is the standard deviation of the feature.

A negative z-score indicates that the data point is below the mean.

A positive z-score indicates that the data point is above the mean.

Data Modelling

Data modeling is the process of creating a visual representation of either a whole information system or parts of it to communicate connections between data points and structures. The goal is to illustrate the types of data used and stored within the system, the relationships among these data types, the ways the data can be grouped and organized and its formats and attributes. Data models are built around business needs.

Model Training and Feature Engineering

A sample data is collected from the main data set. The data is used to train the model in predicting. It is necessary to iterate the data many times so that accurate results can be generated.

Deploying Models to Production

All work to this point culminates in the final step of deploying a model to production where the ability to predict outcomes in the real world is tested. By this point, models should meet some threshold of accuracy that warrants deploying them to production.

How is AI used in our Everyday Life

- Phone with Face recognition
- Social Media platform
- Send an email or message
- Doing Google search
- Digital voice assistants
- Smart home devices
- Commuting
- Banking
- Shopping Recommendations
- Healthcare and Medical
- Logistic Supply Chain
- Imaging Analysis

Some AI Applications in Space Industry

Navigating Rovers on Mars and Moon

Moving Rovers on Mars is a Challenge. Due to the various obstacles, on the surface of Mars in form of Rocks uneven surface. There is a time Lag of 3 to 22 Minutes for one way communication. So the Rovers cannot be controlled real Time from Earth. The best way around this was to let the rover decide the best possible way to reach a particular point avoiding objects and taking the shortest path. They did this using AI. They trained AI with millions of images and then used neural networks to create a virtual map. So that the Rover can take independent decisions of it movement.

Discovery of Kepler Exoplanets

Scientists have used data from NASA's Kepler Space Telescope to find transiting exoplanets. In its extended K2 mission, Kepler observed stars in various regions of sky all across the ecliptic plane. The problem was for the Astronomers wanted to learn how the population of exoplanets are different in these different environments. However, this required an automatic and non-partisan way to identify the exoplanets within these regions and rule out false positive signals that mimic transiting planet signals. To overcome this we they used a deep learning algorithm used in medical fields. They made changes to a neural network that was used to identify exoplanets in different K2 campaigns that range in galactic environments and called it AstroNetK2.It can predict whether a given possible exoplanet signal is really caused by an exoplanet or a false positive. It achieved an accuracy on 98% on the test set. But it still requires human intervention.

Space Debris Solution

 Every year a lot of new satellites are launched .A lot of the previously launched satellites reach their end of life and become space junk. There are more than 23,000 human made fragments in space that are bigger than 4 inch and more than 500000 small particles. These travel with high velocities around the earth .So even if a small debris object hits a satellite it makes a huge dent on the body. To overcome this scientists are using deep learning to accurately pinpoint the location of the debris, they use a technique called backpropagation. Backpropagation is the central mechanism by which neural networks learn. It is the messenger telling the network whether or not the net made a mistake when it made a prediction. Using this technique space debris with a cross-sectional area of 1 meter squared and a distance of 1500 kilometers can be identified accurately.

How will AI affect our future?

AI will create 58 million new artificial intelligence jobs by 2022. There is an excellent chance that by 2030 AI will outperform humans in most of the mental tasks but that does not mean it will take away jobs. Relearning will be required to Keep Jobs.

Ways AI will change the world by 2050

Education:
 Paper Textbooks replaced by digital ones. The Digital books will be smart enough to know whether a student is bored or interested in reading. The digital books will be capable of modifying textbook content as per individual student needs.

Customer Service:
AI assistance that can directly make appointments at your neighborhood salon for haircut .Adding emotional touch to the way AI will speak to customers.

Entertainment:
Customized Movies as per your likings. With human Actors being replaced by virtual ones. Predictive analysis to forecast if a particular script will work in Box Office

Cybersecurity:
With AIs self-learning and Automation Capability AI can protect Data more systematically and affordabaly.AI based tools can look for patterns associated with malicious software before they can Steal information.

Climate:
 Better Climate prediction for changes in weather. Providing information on preparing the land, applying fertilizer and choosing sowing dates. Identifying tropical cyclones. By improving weather forecasts, these types of programs can help keep people safe.

Making cities more livable and sustainable:
 AI can also improve energy efficiency on the city scale by incorporating data from smart meters and the Internet of Things to forecast energy demand. Thereby reducing Pollution.

Potential AI Risks

Performance:

The conclusions of AI may not be understandable to humans. It will be difficult to judge if it's correct or not .AI Deep learning could be risky for applications such as early warning systems for natural disasters where more certainty is needed.

Security:

AI could potentially be hacked. As systems increasingly depend on automation for control, anyone hacking the system can interfere with energy, transportation, early warning or other crucial systems.

Control Risk:

Since AI systems interact autonomously, they can produce unpredictable outcomes. For example, two systems came up with a language of their own that humans couldn't understand. Economic Risks:

Companies that are slower to adopt AI may suffer economic consequences as their AI-based competition advances. We are already seeing rise of Ecommerce and many brick and motor stores closing.

Social Risks:

Job loss in every field will be there as AI will take over routine tasks. Autonomous weapon systems could also hasten and exacerbate global conflicts. Reskilling will be required.

Ethical Risks:

Since AI uses inferred assumptions about groups and communities in making decisions, it could lead to increased bias. The collection of data also raises privacy issues.

This is the 6 x 9 Basic Template. Paste your manuscript into this template or simply start typing. Delete this text prior to use.